Natural Disasters

Droughts

Louise Park

Smart Apple Media

This edition first published in 2008 in the United States of America by Smart Apple Media.

Smart Apple Media
2140 Howard Drive West
North Mankato, Minnesota 56003

First published in 2007 by
MACMILLAN EDUCATION AUSTRALIA PTY LTD
627 Chapel Street, South Yarra, Australia 3141

Visit our Web site at www.macmillan.com.au or go directly to www.macmillanlibrary.com.au

Associated companies and representatives throughout the world.

Library of Congress Cataloging-in-Publication Data

Park, Louise.
    Droughts / by Louise Park.
    p. cm. – (Natural disasters)
    Includes index.
    ISBN 978-1-59920-113-9
    1. Droughts–Juvenile literature. 2. Natural disasters–Juvenile literature. I. Title.

    QC929.25.P37 2007
    551.57'73–dc22

                                                    2007004659

Edited by Sam Munday and Erin Richards
Text and cover design by Ivan Finnegan, iF design
Page layout by Ivan Finnegan, iF design
Photo research by Jes Senbergs
Illustrations by Andy Craig and Nives Porcellato, p. 14
Maps by designscope, pp. 11, 12, 20, 26

Printed in U.S.

Acknowledgements

The author and the publisher are grateful to the following for permission to reproduce copyright material:
Front cover photograph: dry, cracked bed of Lake Eppalock in Victoria, Australia, courtesy of FairfaxPhotos/Jason South.

Background textures courtesy of Ivan Finnegan, iF design.

Lynsey Addario/Corbis, p. 27; AFP/Getty Images, p. 26; Mike Boyatt/Agstock/Science Photo Library, p. 16; Coo-ee Picture Library, pp. 4, 7, 9, 25; FairfaxPhotos/Nick Moir, p. 18; FairfaxPhotos/Jason South, pp. 1, 5; FairfaxPhotos/The Age Archives, p. 8; NASA/Science Photo Library, p. 22; Katie Nguyen/Reuters/Corbis, p.15; NOAA, pp. 21, 23; NOAA/Science Photo Library, p. 20; David Noble Photography/Alamy, p. 10; Alain Nogues/CORBIS SYGMA, p. 17; Alain Nogues/Sygma/Corbis, p. 13; Christine Osborne Pictures/Alamy, p. 12; South Library of South Australia, p. 19; Wendy Stone /Corbis, p. 24; Dieter Telemans /MSF, pp. 6, 28, 29.

Contents

GLOSSARY WORDS

When a word is printed in **bold**, you can look up its meaning in the glossary on page 31.

Natural disasters

Natural disasters are events that occur naturally. They are not caused by human action. They can happen all over the world at any time. When natural disasters occur in populated areas, they can result in death, injury, and damage to property.

Types of natural disasters

There are many types of natural disasters, such as tornadoes, wildfires, droughts, and earthquakes. Each type occurs for very different reasons and affects Earth in different ways. Although they are different, they all create chaos and bring **devastation** and destruction with them wherever they strike.

This soil has been ruined as a result of drought.

Droughts

Droughts are natural disasters. They can dry out the soil and ruin crops and land used for grazing animals. Droughts can cause rivers to run completely dry. They can disturb vital water supplies and cause cattle and livestock to perish. Droughts can be unpredictable and can last for years. When droughts affect an area badly it can be the worst natural disaster of all.

Of all the disasters, drought can be the most costly. Other disasters, such as earthquakes and tornadoes, strike, wreak havoc, and then finish quickly. Drought, however, can affect an area for years. These droughts can have a major impact on the national economy. They can also bring about other disastrous events, such as fires and dust storms.

Disastrous droughts are a natural part of Earth's weather patterns, but what are they and why do we have them?

This freshwater lake in Australia has dried up completely because of drought.

What is drought?

Drought is an unusually long spell of dry weather. This can happen because there has not been enough rainfall, or less rainfall than expected, over a long time. It can also happen when water supplies in dams and rivers dry up from periods of prolonged heat. The effects of drought can be different depending on where it strikes. It can affect water and food supplies, farming, and livestock, and cause serious problems such as **malnutrition** and **famine**. The worst effects of drought occur when there are extremely long spells of dry weather.

Drought can occur in almost all **climatic zones** around the world, but its characteristics vary significantly among regions. Its impact comes from both the natural weather event and from human demands on our water supplies.

Animals cannot survive without fresh water.

When things dry up

When there is not enough rain, and water supplies are below normal, disaster strikes. Water keeps the soil rich and healthy for growing crops. Water also enables natural grasses to grow. These natural grasses help keep the soil in place. Without natural grasses, the soil can dry up and blow away during times of drought. When natural **vegetation** dries out, it can burn easily and fuel fires.

Farmers rely on water to feed animals and grow crops. When there is little or no rainfall, it becomes extremely difficult to grow crops. As the land dries up, so do the land's natural grasses, so animals have less and less to graze on. Rainfall is critical.

Regular rainfall means healthy grazing land and healthy livestock.

DISASTER FILE

Australia

WHAT	One of the worst droughts of the 1900s
WHERE	Eastern Australia
WHEN	1982–83

The drought began in 1982 after poor rainfalls during fall and winter. In just one year, water shortages were so bad that Australia suffered one of the worst droughts of the 1900s.

Eastern Australia suffered extreme heat, a dry spell, failed crops, land devastation, and disastrous wildfires. Many farmers could not keep their livestock alive. They shot them rather than let them suffer.

Think about it

The dust storms from wildfires took weeks to go away. They were so thick that drivers had to use headlights during the day.

Thick dust storms engulfed the city of Melbourne.

Why did it happen?

So many scientists believe that this drought was caused by **El Niño** that it has become known as the "El Niño Drought." El Niño brought the driest eleven-month period on record to Australia.

Counting the cost

Worse was to come as a result of the drought. The Ash Wednesday wildfires broke out on February 16, 1983. These fires were so severe that fire fighters were unable to stop them. The fires only came to an end when they hit the ocean. The wildfires took the lives of 75 people including 17 fire fighters. Over 2,500 homes were lost.

DID YOU KNOW?
The Ash Wednesday wildfires burned through more than 811 square miles (2,100 square km) in Victoria and 803 s miles (2,080 square km) in South Austra. At its biggest, the fire was reported to b moving at over 60 miles (100 km) an hour.

The Ash Wednesday wildfires ran up costs of around $40 million.

Different types of droughts

There are different types of drought that can affect different parts of Earth. Deserts are areas of permanent drought that get little or no rainfall in any given year. Seasonal drought occurs in places that get rain but tend to be very dry for most of the year. Unpredictable drought occurs when rainfall stops for long periods of time. Invisible drought has rainfall that is infrequent and inadequate.

Meteorologists group these types of droughts into three main classifications:

- When there is much less rainfall than needed for a specific period, it is meteorological.

- When there is a reduction in water supplies such as dams, streams, rivers, and lakes, it is hydrological.

- When both meteorological and hydrological types affect crops and farming, it is agricultural.

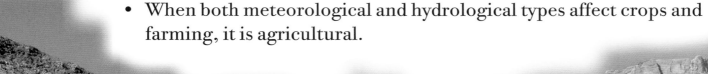

The Mojave Desert in the United States receives little or no rainfall each year.

Where does drought occur?

Most countries have experienced drought or its effects. However, droughts tend to be more severe where Earth is naturally hot. Hot, **arid** climates suffer the worst from drought. The ground here tends to be so dry that when rain does fall, it is quickly absorbed into the ground or blown away by the dry air that moves along the ground.

Africa

Africa has suffered more than any other location from drought disaster. This **continent** has a long history of unpredictable rainfall. When drought hits here, it can last for several years. These severe droughts often cause devastating water and food shortages.

Think about it

Most of North Africa is covered by the largest desert in the world. The Sahara Desert is so big that it splits Africa into two regions. Each year, the edge of the Sahara Desert extends about 3.1 miles (5 km) south.

This map shows the world's most common drought areas.

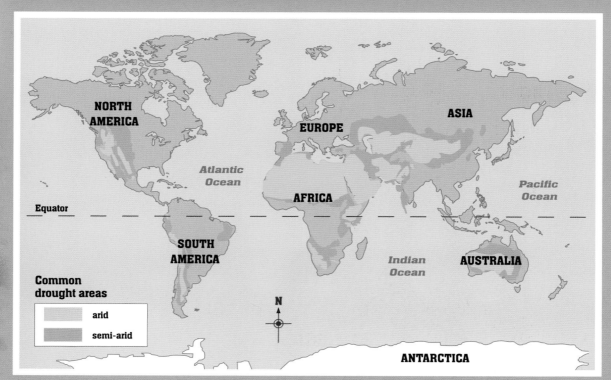

NORTH AMERICA

EUROPE

ASIA

Atlantic Ocean

AFRICA

Pacific Ocean

Equator

SOUTH AMERICA

Indian Ocean

AUSTRALIA

N

Common drought areas

arid

semi-arid

ANTARCTICA

DISASTER FILE
Sahel, Africa

WHAT	The longest period of drought
WHERE	Across the Sahel, Africa
WHEN	1967–88

The Sahel is a **semi-arid** region of Africa, south of the Sahara Desert. The Sahel was hit by two severe droughts during the 1970s and 1980s. However, the entire period from 1967–88 had far less rainfall than was needed. From a meteorological perspective, the Sahel suffered drought for two decades.

In 1971, after four years of poor rainfall, Lake Chad had shrunk to one third of its normal size. In 1972, the Sahel's crops failed and a disastrous food shortage gripped the area. Between 1972 and 1975, more than 600,000 people died. During the second severe drought between 1984 and 1985, nearly one million people died of starvation and disease.

DID YOU KNOW?
In 1973, both North and South Africa were affected by drought. During this time almost every African country suffered. Sixty-one territories and 12 percent of the world's population were affected by this drought in some way.

Refugees who fled drought-stricken areas relied on aid in refugee camps.

Why did it happen?

Irregular rainfalls and no rain at all for long periods caused this disastrous drought. In winter, the Sahel suffers from northeast **trade winds**, which are hot and dry as a result of their long journey over the desert. Because of this, rain is rare or does not occur at all. The dry season grows longer toward the northern part of the Sahel as the Sahara Desert grows bigger each year. In normal years, there is just enough seasonal rainfall to grow crops that can survive through mild droughts. But when years of dry spells occur, crops and livestock perish.

Counting the cost

During the course of the drought, livestock perished and people began walking hundreds of miles in search of food and water. In the early 1980s, another series of poor rainfall years struck most of Africa. By 1984, around three million people in 22 countries were in need of help and food aid.

People in the Sahel know that when crops and livestock perish, people will be next to die.

What causes drought?

Drought is generally caused by a shortage of rainfall. Rainfall is created and distributed around Earth as part of the natural water cycle. When this cycle is disrupted and rain cannot be produced, drought occurs.

As the sun and warm air heat Earth, water **evaporates** into **water vapor**. Water vapor is an invisible gas that rises up into the **atmosphere.** As the vapor rises, it cools, collects, and **condenses** into water droplets to form clouds. Then it falls back to the Earth as rain, hail, or snow.

However, when there are constant **high pressure areas**, moisture cannot be held and clouds cannot form. The result is little or no rainfall, which causes a drought. Normally, high pressure areas move on and are replaced by **low pressure areas**. Sometimes this does not happen and high pressure areas are stalled.

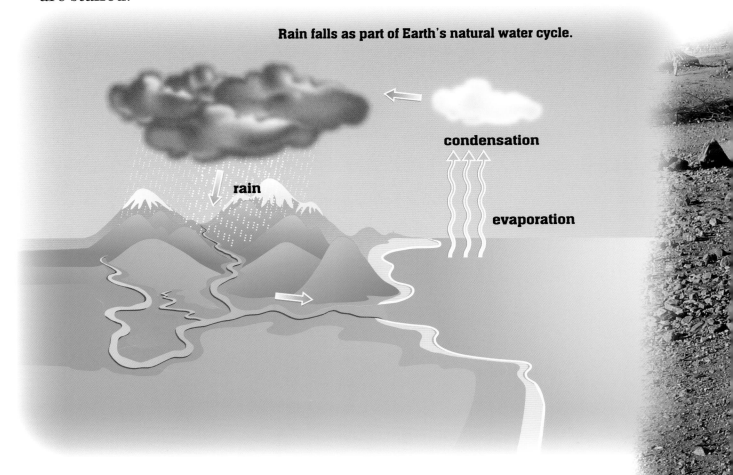

Rain falls as part of Earth's natural water cycle.

condensation

evaporation

rain

El Niño

El Niño is a weather condition that can wreak havoc. El Niño is a disruption of the ocean-atmosphere system in the tropical Pacific. When it occurs, it affects weather all around the world. During an El Niño, the warm currents normally in the southwest Pacific move toward the center of the ocean. This creates drastic changes in weather patterns.

El Niños can have devastating results. Scientists who study the weather believe that many of the droughts in tropical regions are associated with El Niño. El Niños have also been the causes of other natural disasters such as wildfires, hurricanes, floods, and severe storms.

Think about it
El Niño conditions brought about one of the worst droughts in the Horn of Africa.

People in the Horn of Africa continue to suffer food shortages because of drought.

Effects of drought

Water is a crucial part of life. Without it, we would struggle to survive. When drought grips a country, the effects can be devastating. Drought can have environmental, social, and economic impacts depending on the extent of the drought.

Environmental impacts

When the environment begins to dry out, it can put stress on wildlife as well as land. Lack of food and drinking water affects animals as well. Some animals might migrate to other areas. Others may contract disease or starve. As reservoirs, wetlands, and lakes dry up, fish, birdlife, and other species struggle to survive and may become endangered. At the same time, erosion of soil and poor soil quality make it impossible to grow crops. Plant life and vegetation also struggle to survive in these conditions.

Crops fail when there is little or no water.

Social impacts

Serious drought can have many social impacts. In some countries, people move to other places in search of land where they can survive. This happened during a drought in the Horn of Africa in 1984. This drought drove 2.5 million people in the region to abandon their homes and flee to neighboring countries. Severe drought can also cause deaths, famine, and loss of animals, crops, and livelihood.

Economic impacts

When drought strikes, the resources of the country suffer as well as the people. Farmers may lose money if a drought destroys their crops. They might also lose livestock, or need to spend more money on food and water for them. Businesses can also be affected by drought. Tractor and food manufacturers lose business when crops and livestock are reduced.

Thousands of refugees flee the Horn of Africa in search of food and water.

Fires and dust storms

When hot, dry winds blow during a drought, they can cause fires and dust storms.

Fires

Drought can cause fires to break out. When there is plenty of rain, the environment is lush and green. When there is no rain for a long period, the environment becomes dry and the perfect fuel for a fire. Not all fire breakouts are disastrous—some fires may just burn through grasses. Other wildfires can be so bad they are like firestorms. These fires come with strong, hot winds. They can destroy vegetation, land, animals, homes, and anything else that the fire can feed on. It can take years for the land to recover from disastrous fires like these.

DID YOU KNOW?
Sometimes fires are started by people to clear the land of undergrowth. This is done so that there is less fuel for a wildfire to burn if one breaks out. This is called controlled burning.

Strong winds can push fires along at alarming speeds.

Dust storms

When winds blow during droughts, they can create dust storms. Winds pick up dry topsoil and blow it into huge, dark clouds that can travel hundreds of miles. Tons of topsoil can be carried away and dropped by dust storms. These storms can destroy croplands and damage trees and houses. Severe dust storms can make it impossible to drive. They are a serious hazard in times of drought.

Think about it

Australia had one of its worst dust storms in the state of South Australia during 1944. The dust storm carried away 24 million tons of topsoil. That's enough soil to fill 100 football stadiums.

The dust storms in South Australia in 1944 turned day into night.

DISASTER FILE
Dust Bowl, United States

WHAT	The worst drought with dust storms in U.S. history
WHERE	United States
WHEN	1931–39

The U.S. suffered a severe drought that lasted from 1931–39. This drought brought some of the worst dust storms ever seen. The whole affected area became known as the Dust Bowl as a result. At the height of the drought in 1934, 75 percent of the United States was affected.

The Dust Bowl drought was a natural disaster that came in three waves: 1934, 1936, and 1939. However, some regions experienced drought conditions for up to eight years. During this drought, the soil of the Great Plains dried out, turned to dust, and blew away.

The soil of the Great Plains blew away in devastating dust storms.

The dust storms buried entire buildings in sand and dust.

Why did it happen?

Too much demand on the land and poor rainfall caused the Dust Bowl. The Great Plains was heavily plowed and planted. With healthy rainfalls, farmers could meet increasing demands for crops. When the droughts hit and took hold, farmers kept plowing and planting, stripping away the natural vegetation. There was nothing left to hold the soil in place and it was exposed. The soil dried out and was blown away in extreme dust storms.

Counting the cost

This disaster left over 500,000 people homeless. More than 78,000 square miles (202,000 sq km) of land were destroyed by the effects of the Dust Bowl. Dust storms carried enormous amounts of dirt from one place to another. Those caught in the dust storms were left either dead or with damaged airways from dust inhalation. Animals also perished because of the dust they consumed. Cars were destroyed, along with homes and barns, as they filled with dust and sand.

Measuring drought

It can be hard to tell when drought begins and ends. For this reason, careful monitoring of the causes of drought is important. Meteorologists measure the amount of rainfall. Studies of the land and its dryness are also carried out.

Using satellites

Meteorologists use satellite images to observe weather patterns around the world. Images are taken regularly and comparisons made of the same areas over time. Combining this information with other measurements allows scientists to accurately predict some droughts.

Measurement indexes

Measurement indexes have been developed by some countries where drought is not uncommon. Most of the United States uses the Palmer Drought Severity Index to assess drought conditions. It ranks areas into one of four drought conditions: abnormally dry (-1 to -1.9), moderate drought (-2 to -2.9), severe drought (-3 to -3.9), and extreme drought (-4.0).

Examining satellite pictures of water levels can help scientists predict drought.

Global monitoring

Although many countries have developed their own measurement indexes, it is important to have a world view. Meteorologists need up-to-date information on global weather patterns. The World Meteorological Organization gathers information from countries all around the world. They study this information and issue reports to their members.

U.S. drought declaration

In the U.S., drought can be declared by either Federal or State government. They look at rainfall information and weather patterns from the National Weather Service before deciding whether to declare a drought.

The World Meteorological Organization plays an important role in world drought prediction.

Managing drought

There are areas of the world where drought is frequent. Here, communities are more experienced in surviving years of drought. Looking after land and water can minimize the effects of drought.

Soil conservation

In Africa, it is very hard to keep dry land **fertile** enough to grow crops. Farmland is used for growing crops for three-year periods. During this time, all the nutrients in the soil get used up. Farmers now know to leave this land crop-free for the next seven or eight years. This gives the soil a chance to replenish with nutrients.

Clearing trees and natural grasses worsens the effects of drought. Keeping this vegetation keeps moisture in the soil. In Ethiopia, most of the forests were cut down. Trees were used to make and sell lumber. Ethiopia now has a huge reforestation program. Reclaiming natural forests will significantly lessen the effects of drought.

Tree felling in Ethiopia in the past contributed to the effects of drought.

Water conservation

Fresh water is our most precious resource. Conserving water is vital. Using up water that is not being replaced during times of drought can take its toll. The hot conditions that come with drought also bring high levels of evaporation to already depleted water supplies. For water to last longer, restrictions are often placed on water usage.

The conservation of water is vital in times of drought.

DISASTER FILE
Rajasthan, India

WHAT	Worst land and crop devastation ever caused by drought
WHERE	Across 31 districts in Rajasthan, India
WHEN	1998–2001

Rajasthan is the largest state in India. During this severe drought, 31 of its 32 districts were significantly affected.

Thirty-four million of the 44 million people in Rajasthan live in rural areas. The drought meant that crops and cattle suffered disastrously. Of the 2,647 major water reservoirs in Rajasthan, only 300 of these were filled during the drought. Other reservoirs all but dried up, waiting for rain that did not come. Water supplies to cities, towns, and villages were cut off by this shortage of rainfall. Between 75 and 100 percent of crops failed as a result of a lack of water. People and cattle began migrating in search of food and water.

Rajasthan's water reservoirs were almost empty as a result of the drought.

Why did it happen?

Rajasthan is an arid and semi-arid region. Rainfall is extremely erratic and unpredictable. Unpredictable rainfall affects water resources. During this drought, Rajasthan did not have a normal monsoon season. Instead, it suffered from several very dry spells. During this time, Rajasthan received only around a third of the rainfall it needed.

Counting the cost

The estimated loss in crops alone was around $800 million. Approximately 40 million people and 50 million cattle were left devastated by this drought.

Many people traveled long distances in search of fresh water.

Think about it

Some villages had absolutely no water at all during this drought. Once ever two weeks a tanker provided village with about 2.6 gallons (10 l) of water each.

Disaster relief

Severe drought can devastate communities. People are often displaced as a result of drought. The first step is to help victims who have lost their homes and livelihood to drought. Areas are set up where relief can be provided to victims. People who have suffered the effects of a drought often need shelter, food, and fresh water.

After relief efforts have been established, governments begin the work of rehabilitation. Funds are provided for farming equipment, new crops, and water supplies. Governments also provide financial assistance to people in times of drought. Help is given to farmers carrying debts and who may be suffering from lack of income as a result of drought. Small businesses are also given financial support to see them through these hard times.

Aid workers provide fresh water to people in drought-stricken Somalia.

Living with drought

Drought is a global issue that needs to be taken seriously. Changes in global weather patterns could mean more and more extreme disasters. As our cities grow bigger and bigger, the amount of water we use increases. Saving water needs to be a natural way of life. Water conservation is important every day, not just in times of drought.

DID YOU KNOW?

Some scientists believe climate change or global warming may be causes of severe droughts. Studies have found that higher temperatures caused significant increases in the evaporation of water. Global temperatures have increased over the past 50 years as a result of industrial gases being released into our atmosphere.

Children are among the first casualties during drought.

DISASTER FILES AT A GLANCE

The four droughts profiled in this book are record-breaking for different reasons. This graph shows the scale of each of them.

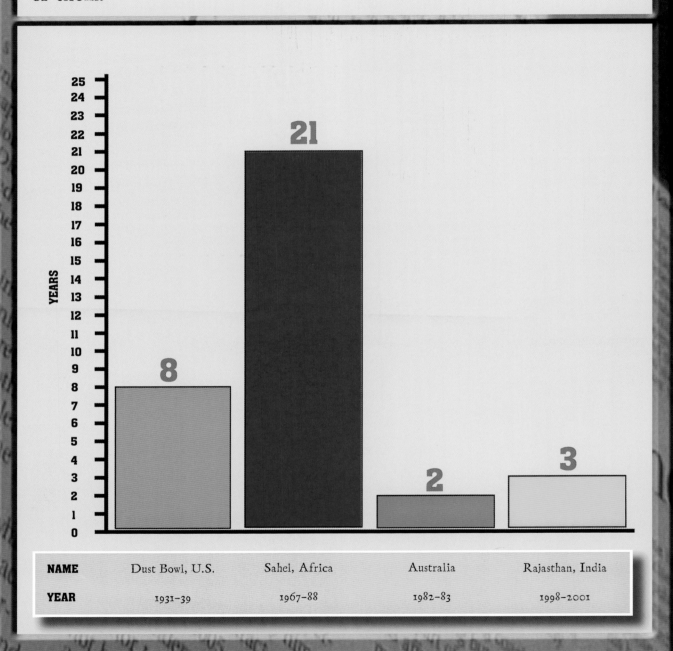

NAME	Dust Bowl, U.S.	Sahel, Africa	Australia	Rajasthan, India
YEAR	1931–39	1967–88	1982–83	1998–2001

Glossary

arid	area with little or no moisture, such as a desert
atmosphere	blanket of gases that surrounds Earth
climatic zones	regions of the world divided according to their usual annual rainfalls
condenses	when gas changes into liquid
continent	major land mass on Earth
devastation	severe damage or destruction
El Niño	abnormal warming of surface waters in the tropical Pacific, which causes changes in weather patterns
evaporates	when liquid changes into gas
famine	drastic and wide-reaching food shortage
fertile	rich in nutrients that crops need to grow
high pressure areas	large areas of cool, dry air
low pressure areas	large areas of warm, humid air
malnutrition	poor health from lack of food
meteorologists	scientists who study weather patterns
semi-arid	area that receives low annual rainfalls
trade winds	continuous tropical winds that move toward the Equator, from the northeast in the Northern Hemisphere and the southeast in the Southern Hemisphere
vegetation	the plants of an area
water vapor	water as a gas

Index